pain.

Marigold Beaumont

Presentation by *BookLeaf Publishing*

Web: www.bookleafpub.com

E-mail: info@bookleafpub.com

ISBN: 9789357442572

First edition 2023

*to my mom as she's the only one who didn't
break my heart.*

these words

These words that are playing in my head,
Filling my mind with so much dread.
On the loop, always on repeat,
Like a record player never missing a beat.

These words that hold so much meaning,
I hear them only when you're screaming.
Is this the way people raise their kids?
Bottling up the feelings and closing the lids.

These words I learned when I was three,
So strongly embedded in my memory.
Hereby I believe I cannot be adored,
Until my looks don't make you feel bored.

These words have ruined my life,
So many times I've reached for that knife.
Hand trembling, steady enough not to drop,
It's something sharp that will make it all stop.

These words of yours that have hurt me,
And endless times that I have told thee,
You chose to be ignorant and ungracious,
Yet wonder how I am so ambitious…

To get away from these words you have spoken,
The bond between us is long broken.
But I hope that one day you will understand,
My forgiveness is something you can never land.

silent hopes

The light is leaving.
His eyes tired, revealing,
How long the journey has been,
Losing to light is now a win.

I see how scared you are of being gone,
For me, you are still holding on.
Don't go through to avoid my pain,
Letting go will not be in vain.

I have many hours to feel the ache,
Don't waste your minutes for my sake.
I ain't worthy of your time,
Please, don't give me a single dime.

You were the first to leave,
And I couldn't even grieve.
I may have chosen to disconnect,
But you will always have my respect.

The guilt I feel I shall keep with me,
To remind of who I don't want to be.
Beyond the sky and ground I seek thee,
In silent hopes you forgive me.

you burned me

Gave me a breath to follow your law,
Yet, afraid of treasures I could claw.
Don't speak too loud or climb too high,
You rather burn me and hear me cry.

Stay in your box to learn and grow,
Knowing well a square cannot glow.
Do what you're told, and you'll succeed,
Asking me to trust your mislead.

Your words are like whips that scar my heart,
But I refuse to play this part.
A role where my purpose is to please the greater
good,
Blindly follow a view that's misunderstood.

Your good is different from mine,
Your good is something you designed.
Your good is no good at all,
Your good makes people feel small.

You burned me for many years,
You exposed my biggest fears.
These scars I shall return,
And now I will watch you burn.

teardrops

5

It's in the teardrops the story unfolds.
Smug and heavy,
or light, without its heat.
A waterfall waiting what it beholds,
Ray of sadness,
Blurred lines following the beat.
A heavy stone laying on heart,
Unable to start
Pumping.
Laying, broken apart.
Is this what you call art?
The nerve, the torture, the pain,
Why do I feel such strain?
Breathe.
Breathe.
Take one breath, then another.
God, I sound like my mother.
It's in my teardrops the secret unfolds,
I am not ready for what it beholds.

broken

I can't sleep
I see nightmares and dreams
And wake up tired
As if living another life
In the darkest hours of the day
I can't get out of bed
When I have nowhere to be
The light inside me
Turns off on my days off
I curl into a ball
Tangled in sheets
While everything feels
Tragic
I can't keep going like this
Living day by day
Wondering if I will have enough
To put on a table the next day
Month to month
I stress about little things
Nobody told me
That living is harder
Than not
Nothing can go astray
Or I will not have a way
To get out of the bottom

I have wasted my wrinkles
To survive in a world
That is not fit for young eyes
Or dreams and passions
And anything that makes me happy
I am doomed to sadness
To little stresses
To life without pleasures
No one by my side
No one who understands
How hard I have tried
Not to be where I am destined to be
Tired
Of moving, loving, living
Give me a break
As I'm already broken.

black hole

There's this little tingling feeling in my chest,
It appears especially when I'm stressed.
It lays heavily on my heart,
Bit by bit tearing me apart.

I cannot explain where it comes from,
Or why it leaves me feeling numb.
It can appear out of nowhere,
And linger around me in the air.

It makes me afraid when I feel it,
Because I can never truly control it.
It makes me do things that may cause harm,
Setting the fire where there's no smoke alarm.

Whenever it comes I tend to run away,
So no one can ever hear me say,
All the nasty things I have on my mind,
Because this feeling has never been kind.

It overwhelms my body and takes possession,
I feel like I'm unwillingly slipping into
depression.
And once it has total control,
It sends my soul to live in a black hole.

place to call home

It's that time of the year where winter ends,
And it tests my loyalties with my friends.
It's that time I must decide,
If for one more year,
They'll be my ride or die.

I'd say it's something deep and wise,
But we live in a city,
Where the cost of living is always on the rise.
I am waiting for the message from my landlord,
Asking if the flat is something I can still afford.

I am sick and tired of moving every single year,
I just want a place where I can live without fear.
But here I am once again in panic,
Hoping my friend doesn't drown us
Like we'd be passengers on Titanic.

I have to admit that I am scared,
Because this was a dream that we once shared.
I know that it's something we can still achieve,
I want to stay and fight but she wants to leave.

At the end of the day, I might be left alone,
Fighting for my life to the absolute bone.
There is not enough money in my account,
No one will be able to help me,
Not with that much amount.

Is it too much to ask to have something nice,
Without paying the rent double in price.
I'm not asking for much,
I don't need to live in the centre of Rome.
I just want a place that I can call home.

stars

The Moon and the Sun did not shine today,
Letting the Stars guide their own way.
Going in circles around the bay,
Slowly throwing their blossoming away.

The Sun and the Moon did not dance tonight,
Building a path for their ice-cold fight.
Leaving the Stars alone to shine bright,
Affirming that everything will be alright.

The Moon convinced it lost its voice,
But the Stars gave it one last choice:
Sing to the Sun with all your heart,
Giving love is a damn good start.

companion

I find myself in the same predicament
That ended my time with another friend.
A simple minded boy
Became my companion's new toy.

It's different for her but the same for me,
A story I never wanted to repeat.
I wouldn't change how I reacted,
But I will always regret how it ended.

I miss you my old friend,
I thought it could be us until the end.
Maybe not as close as we once were,
But somewhere where these lines do blur.

I am scared the history will repeat itself,
And I'll be placed back on the shelf.
Picked up like a book you don't want to read,
Wiping away dust like it's a good deed.

I'm trying to be good and be on his team,
But it's again the same fucking theme.
I go against what I feel is right,
To keep a friendship out of fight.

But then you turn around and tell me to
compete,
With someone who's already in the lead.
You've had my love for many years,
Yet choose a stranger over your companion's
tears.

dreams

Laziness is a set of mind,
Not a burden that makes you blind.
It is a habit you train,
That forever alters your brain.

You can choose to let it overtake your day,
Raise your hands above your head and pray:
That one day it will go away,
But it's you who has the say.

You cannot tell it to stop,
You can only force it to drop.
Get up and live your life the way you want,
These dreams of yours you will have to hunt.

Nothing in this world comes for free,
But you can choose who you want to be.
And if that want is stronger than your need,
You will reach the top with incredible speed.

It is not luck or fortune or fame,
But the strength you use to tame
The dreams that live inside,
The dreams you chase with pride.

blood & tears

The blood and tears I have given you,
Sold my soul for your dreams to come true.
Years and years and years went by,
And all you ever do is cry.

You say life is unfair, that you cannot bear
What it's pulling you through,
Do you even have a clue?
A career doesn't come out of the blue.

You work and you work hard,
Protect your heart, be your own best guard.
You fail and you get up,
Never stop reaching for that cup.

The life you've chosen is rough,
Don't let them see your bluff.
It can all go away in one puff,
It will never be enough.

The blood and tears I have given you,
Sold my soul for your dreams to come true.
I say these words as I approach nearer
The person I see in the mirror.

terrible price

I believe underneath I was born to be on stage,
A hope that slowly fades away with my age.
There's still a little fight left in me for the art,
That I've dedicated my whole life and heart.

Twenty years in the making,
And I still can't seem to stop faking:
How much I admire to step in someone's shoes,
To bring a story to life with all its blues.

To paint a world that is not of my own,
Share a journey that has not been known.
Show the world how great it can be,
If we all come together in solidarity.

Sometimes I wonder if I'm truly loyal,
Or if I just want to become a royal.
So many people seeking fortune and fame,
What if someday I forget my true aim?

No matter how much your heart wants to be
good,
This industry has destroyed it as best as it could.
Toughen your heart to be made of ice,
Life as an artist has a terrible price.

devil's crown

Look up at the sky,
And you shall burn your eye.
There's someone sitting high,
Someone who will make you cry.

He is watching over the town,
From his cloud, looking down.
On his head sits a devil's crown,
His face - painted like a clown.

Common folk don't hear him scream and shout,
It's the hierarchy making you doubt,
Pulling lies away from his clout,
Protecting you all from the drought.

A devil's crown shall bring the disease,
A sick mind holding all the keys.
Power is all that he wants to seize,
I beg you, let me help you, please.

Words of wisdom come and go,
He will listen as they snow.
And will agree to make his Kingdom glow,
But don't forget, we live in a Devil's
show.

corporate stage

I spent months preparing for this moment,
Collecting every single component.
This was a matter of work not heart,
I had to be careful and smart.

My seniors look at my young age,
And they tell me to get off that corporate stage.
They say I am far too young to be in charge,
Of a company that is this large.

I did not ask to be on top,
I silently wish this all would stop.
But when I had nowhere to go,
I opened my mouth and asked to know:

Could I get something, or anything more,
Maybe a penny, two or four?
I was not born to beg for mercy,
I much rather cause controversy.

But against all odds here I stood,
And somehow convinced you that I am good.
I swore to make things great and sleek,
I made a promise I could not keep.

A young mind like mine made a mistake,
The ground under my feet started to shake.
My inexperience caused a circus,
Would you believe I didn't do it on purpose?

ghost of my past

I read stories of friendships of others,
From enemies to lovers.
I saw people love and fight,
Sometimes even bite.
I looked upon you,
I adored you,
I cheered for you.
You were my master, I learned from you.
All for you to take me for a fool.
Why did you have to be so cruel?
I thought I would make you proud,
I thought you taught me to be loud.
So, when I finally have the crown,
Why do you try to take it down?
You died of your own choice,
So, why are you still raising your voice?
You know this cannot last.
You are a ghost of my past.

the face I wanted to see

I saw your face in the crowd,
My mind suddenly went loud.
My arm started to reach for yours,
I pulled it back and shut my mental doors.

I saw your face because it's the face I wanted to
see,
Your eyes and lips will forever be engraved in
me.
But as I stared at this person on the chair,
He had the nerve to return my glare.

Disappointment flashed through my eyes,
Maybe a little anger and fury along the lines.
As your face was no longer there,
Faded away in the winter air.

I felt something sink in my chest,
My heart had just confessed.
I wanted us to be through,
But the truth was, I really missed you.

comedic relief

I'm never the girl who gets the guy,
Or the girl who doesn't even have to try,
To be funny and smart and unknowingly pretty,
Turning heads in every single city.

I am the best friend, the one you can't see,
Covered by shadows so I can't disagree.
Don't be too loud, don't cause a scene,
Speak when it's time for comedic relief.

There is no movie where I am the lead,
You'll never see me on the cover of a magazine.
No notes will ever form my name in a song,
Or make me feel like there's a place I belong.

This life has been cruel to me and my kind,
Forced to watch our friends from aside.
As they fall in love, wine and dine,
Get the guy who will never be mine.

My thoughts and opinions are always dismissed,
As I am not the one he would've liked to have
kissed.
My destiny has always been set in stone,
I am the one who ends up alone.

coward

I am a coward.
Sulking in the silk sheets,
Refusing to be devoured
By something that is not real,
But is perhaps the only thing
That will make me feel
Happy.
And a little destroyed at the same time,
It's like walking a very thin line.
To find the diamond in the rough,
You have to go through some stuff
That may break you apart,
But the light at the very end
Will fill your heart
With so much joy and love,
The warmth will fit you like a glove.
The question is simple:
Are you ready to risk it all?
Or forever continue to stall?
If not now then when?
Take a deep breath, count to ten.
Ready, set, and off you go,
Shake the earth with your blow.
But the world stays the same,
As I am a coward,
Afraid to play the game.

the world is on fire

Nothing is fine and the world is on fire,
Burning my back with flames going higher.
My soul is aflame as I wake up and preach,
My friend, my lover,
You're too far away,
I cannot reach.
Chains around my chest squeeze tighter,
As I'm convincing myself I am a fighter.
How can I fight if I am the kind,
That goes to war like blind leading the blind.
The anger, the fury, the absolute rage,
Consumes my skin like a fiery cage.
I'm kicking and yelling about a truce,
I shoot my shot.
Backfire.
Now there's a bruise
On my hand, on my leg, on my back,
Why can I only see black?
Instead of dreams I feel nightmares that crack
Me open like a sack.
Is there something I lack?
Why am I not enough?
I'm so tired of pretending to be tough.
I fall and I rise to fall and rise again,
When will the ink stop bleeding from my pen?

Await the day when I don't need to shout,
When the rain will put my fire out.

25